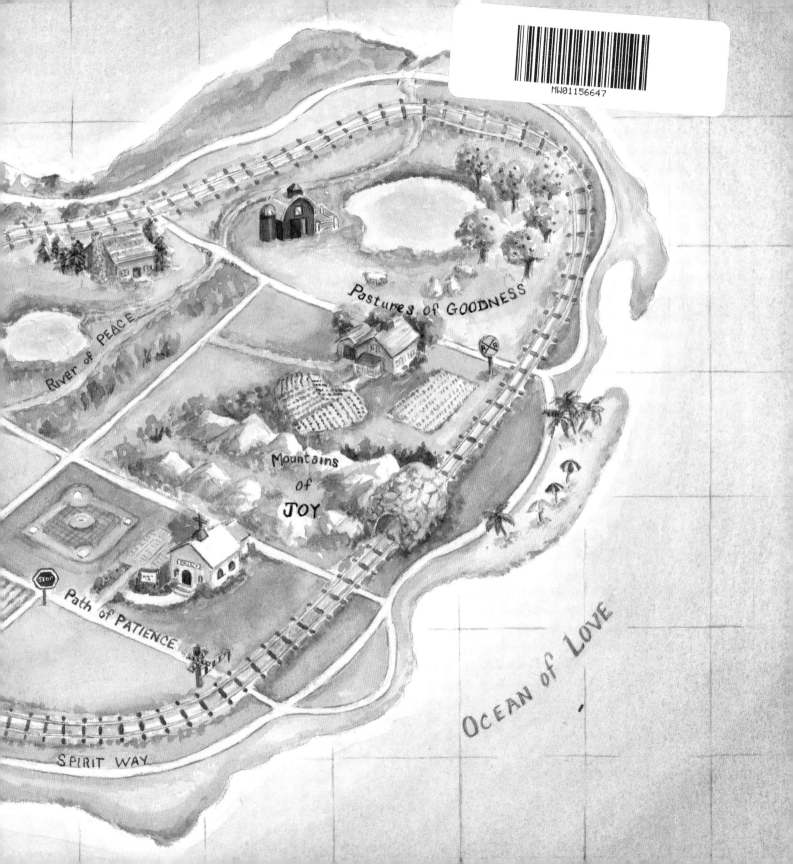

Pastures of GOODNESS

River of PEACE

Mountains
of
JOY

Path of PATIENCE

SPIRIT WAY

Ocean of LOVE

I John 4:7

Love
Faithfulness
Goodness
Joy
JAN 8
Proverbs 3

One Way   THE HEART EXPRESS   Ticket

·ALL ABOARD·

Issued To ....

By ....

On ....

Nᵒ

TRIP of a LIFETIME

Peace
PLACE of REST
Gentleness
trol
Prov 15

A Little Boy After God's Own Heart

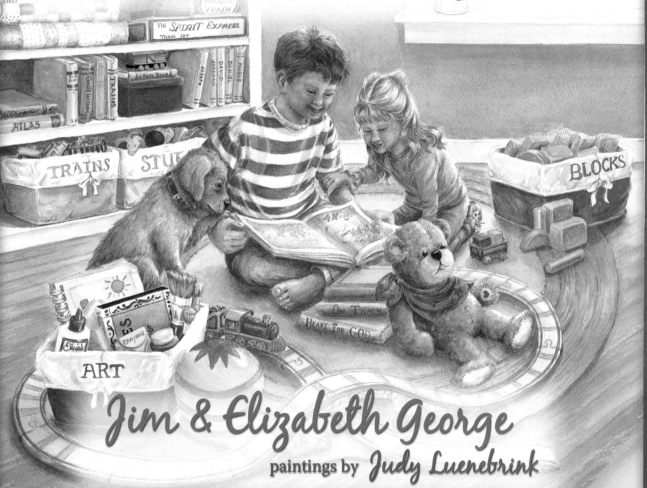

Jim & Elizabeth George

paintings by Judy Luenebrink

HARVEST HOUSE PUBLISHERS
EUGENE, OREGON

A LITTLE BOY AFTER GOD'S OWN HEART

Text copyright © 2007 by Jim and Elizabeth George
Artwork copyright © 2007 by Judy Luenebrink
Published by Harvest House Publishers
Eugene, Oregon 97402

ISBN-13: 978-0-7369-1782-7
ISBN-10: 0-7369-1782-9

Cover and interior by Katie Brady Design and Illustration

Scripture quotations are from *The International Children's Bible*, New Century Version, copyright © 1986 by Word
Publishing, Nashville, Tennessee. Used by permission.

Printed in China

07 08 09 10 11 12 13 14 15 / IM / 10 9 8 7 6 5 4 3 2 1

Jim and Elizabeth George
P.O. Box 2879
Belfair, WA 98528
1-800-542-4611
www.ElizabethGeorge.com
www.JimGeorge.com

Judy Luenebrink
1-818-888-9934
www.judyluenebrink.com

These verses and this book are written for you, our cherished grandsons.
May you always follow after God's heart.

Dear friend,

There is nothing quite as special as a little boy! And there's nothing as rewarding as helping that little boy to blossom and grow in character. In this book you'll find nine qualities that are important for the little boys in your life to know about, and to nurture in their daily lives. Every child struggles with being nice, staying calm, extending kindness, and showing love. But God makes His help and instruction available.

So gather up your little boys and come along. Read about some of the everyday decisions little ones must make. Introduce them to the unchanging scriptures that teach them the right things to do and the right choices to make. Let them see how God's way is always the best way! You'll be delighted as you witness the seed you are planting into precious little hearts begin to bear fruit.

In His everlasting love,

Jim & Elizabeth George

A Heart Filled with...
Love

"Love each other,
because love comes from God."

1 JOHN 4:7

Love

Love comes from God and fills up your heart.
You can share it with others right from the start.
So when someone else asks something of you,
Show them God's love in all that you do.

"Hey, want to come into my room and play?"
Should be your thought toward others each day.
When you're kind and friendly and choose not
    to be mean,
God's love for your pals is lived out and seen.

OCEAN of LOVE

A Heart Filled with...
Joy and Peace

"Be full of joy and
live in peace with each other."

PHILIPPIANS 4:4 AND 1 THESSALONIANS 5:13

Joy and Peace

Sometimes a boy wants to be naughty and fight,
But God says seek peace and do what is right.
True joy is a blessing to those who make peace,
So stop all your fussing and arguing please.

God's peace and joy are what everyone needs,
And a boy with these traits makes a good friend indeed.
"Lord, open my heart to those who are sad.
Let Your joy and peace help them to be glad."

River of PEACE

Mountains of JOY

A Heart Filled with...

Patience

"Be patient with every person."

1 THESSALONIANS 5:14

Patience

"I'm tired of waiting. Speed up! Come on!"
Are the words of a boy whose patience is gone.
How can a guy wait when he's raring to go?
He asks God for patience and help to go slow.

When you're in a hurry, don't think of yourself.
Instead ask the question, "How can I help?"
Let God give you patience for the needs of others,
Including your parents, sisters, and brothers.

Path of PATIENCE

A Heart Filled with...
Kindness and Goodness

"Be kind and do good to people
who need help."

Proverbs 3:27 and Ephesians 4:32

Kindness and Goodness

Kindness is a quality God wants in you,
To be nice to others your whole day through.
Who is in need of your visit today?
Who can you comfort along life's way?

Being good to others is God's Golden Rule,
And His little boys are not to be cruel.
God wants kindness, so tops on your list
Is to spot those in need and quickly assist!

Point of KINDNESS

Pastures of GOODNESS

A Heart Filled with...
Faithfulness

"It is hard to find someone who really can be trusted."

PROVERBS 20:6

Faithfulness

Do you have a job that's been given to you?
Can others count on your following through?
Being part of a family means doing some chores,
Completing your work before playing outdoors.

God's little boy is faithful and true,
So if you promise to help, be sure that you do.
Oh, how a family is happy and blessed
When you, their dear son, show faithfulness.

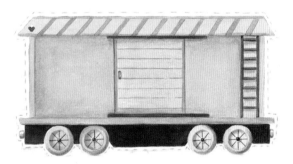

Lighthouse of
FAITHFULNESS

A Heart Filled with...
Gentleness

"Be gentle and polite to all people."

Titus 3:2

Gentleness

Loud, rough, and rowdy describes most little boys.
They run, and they jump, and they scatter their toys.
But God's little boy is way different from these—
He's gentle and calm and puts people at ease.

Gentleness seems strange to an active young guy,
Who thinks being gentle shows weakness inside.
But gentleness is part of God's wonderful plan,
As boys use their strength to help where they can.

GENTLENESS
Harbor

A Heart Filled with...
Self-Control

"Never shout angrily or say things to hurt others. Never do anything evil."

EPHESIANS 4:31

Self-Control

Has something like this ever happened to you?
Your friend rang your doorbell out of the blue.
He wanted to know if you could come out and play,
But when you asked Mom, she said, "No, not today."

At times like this, when you don't get your way,
Self-control's what you need—it alone saves the day!
Before you yell, have a fit, get mad, and attack,
You should stop, pray to God, and decide how to act.

Tracks of SELF-CONTROL

Words to Know

Stingy: doesn't like to share

Deeds: acts of kindness

Blue: sad

Delay: wait, slow down

Regret: be sorry for

Mercy: showing kindness to others

Red-letter day: a very special day

Self-control: calm, even-tempered

Ignite: get angry

Love Joy and Peace

Patience Kindness and Goodness Faithfulness

Gentleness Self-Control

Lighthouse of
FAITHFULNESS

Tracks of SELF-CONTROL

Point
of
KINDNESS

GENTLENESS
Harbor

TRAIN STATION

The
HEART LAND

N
W   E
S